Trash Truck 7:38 A.M.
(And Other Love Poems)

poems by

Ed McManis

Finishing Line Press
Georgetown, Kentucky

Trash Truck 7:38 A.M.
(And Other Love Poems)

ACKNOWLEDGMENTS

Poet Masters Anthology: "Covid Week Four: Ravens": Feb., '23
The Ravensperch: "Underdog" "Trash Truck7:38 A.M." "The Mermaid
Seduction" "Nutcracker": July, '23
Mudfish 18: "Drowsy"
The Ravensperch: "Vigil" "Angels": Oct, '23
Cathexis Northwest: "In the Spirit"
CSPS Quarterly: "Thirtieth Anniversary"

WITH THANKS TO

Marc Z., Gloria M., Linda L., Julie C., Kira P., Steve D., Joe H., Joe Mc.

Publisher: Leah Huete de Maines
Editor: Christen Kincaid
Cover Art and Design: Joe McManis
Author Photo: Linda McManis

Order online: www.finishinglinepress.com
also available on amazon.com

Author inquiries and mail orders:
Finishing Line Press
PO Box 1626
Georgetown, Kentucky 40324
USA

Contents

For Linda

COVID Week Four: Ravens

The crows are circling tighter and tighter,
nine rings of avian hell.
To appease, my wife sets out saltines
on the fence post at eight
and four, as if to feed working shifts.

The first two days, squirrels find
the crackers, scramble down from
the redwoods, tails undulating like parade
banners, nibble, hesitate, left, right—gone.

Then on the third day as if culled
from a page of the Old Testament,
a cacophony rushes me to the window
where she's already a witness.

Four, five, half a dozen, like winged
priests around an altar.
(She tells me later, it's called a *murder*.)
Cawing at the squirrels, pecking, wings
fanned in Kabuki drama—the squirrels retreat.

The following afternoon I spot what looks
like an oil rag in the driveway, stoop
to pick it up, realize it has a tail,
guts exposed, flesh unzipped,
eyes pecked out, neck hanging on.

I don't say anything to her.

The next morning over waffles she announces,
"I think those were ravens.
They looked larger,
the tails wedged."
I "hmm" an agreement. Who studies tails?

"Apparently crows hold grudges," she says,
reaching into the saltine box.
"Probably ravens, too."

We've been married forty years.
"No doubt," I say, ruffling my feathers.
"Maybe add another cracker."

My Grandfather's Marriage
(For P.C.)

Picture the chaste bedroom
silent, dark as the vestibule
of St. Theresa's.

Sarah, in her Sears
nightgown, turns and reaches,
the coupling almost polite,
a quick-step before desire's stoop.

Check. Check.

A whisper or two in the after,
tomorrow's chores, assurance
about the front door—
"Yes, I hooked the chain."

My Parents' Marriage

A shower of rice,
and tin cans wired
to the Ford bumper
chatter like old men
betting on the night
to come.

Starlings pick up
after the wedding
guests hustle
in line for mints.

She is glass still moist
from the press; he trembles
like a choir boy
as the notes crack
beneath the bed.

Black birds gather at dusk
like sacrificial lanterns
along the window ledge.

In the morning she hangs
her spotted sheet to dry;
he winces and feels
for the missing bone beneath
his heart, and the birds,

the birds sleep in
anticipating
a feast.

The Mermaid Seduction

Silver flash of tail,
streak of emerald
beneath a crashing

wave, I first spotted
her swimming alone,
apart from the others

who were swirling
and diving, teasing
a grizzled fisherman.

I wasn't fishing,
just killing time
in my 20s trying

to decide how far in
I should wade, who would
care if I returned to shore.

She circled closer, closer,
breached the glassy surface,
splashed me head-to-foot.

I heard my older brother's
voice, *Don't stare at the
tail.* I focused on the locket

above her breasts, complimented
her scales, casually offered
thoughts on treasure maps,
hot white sand, recent
research on interspecies
attraction, the security

of a monkey knot.
I let her finger the panoply
of intricately tied flies

in my tackle box. As we
settled into each other's myths,
she unhooked the barbs

down my throat to the heart.
I realized time favors the sea,
the green, dying shanties I sing.

The Underdog

I was leafing through the Old
Testament, stopped at David,
wondered if I could whip
a slingshot, find the bulls-eye
on a giant's forehead, watch him drop,
still be a *Christian*.

Maybe I'm more like Job, all life's
injustices sewn into my multi-colored
Joseph-coat of misery, no rabbit's foot
or horseshoe, not enough therapy.

In her inscribed Bible she lives
in the New Testament, highlights
passages of hope and mercy, miracles:
Jesus walks on water, Lazarus
rises, and then Jesus, *his self*,
washes all those pagan feet,

commands us to do the same.
I haven't dared to look at all her
dog-eared pages, not sure I could
survive all that mercy, me sitting
here in the dank pit of the whale's
belly, comfortable in the darkness,
grasping blindly for purchase,
fumbling for smooth stones.

Nutcracker

She cries
at the Nutcracker
when the snow
falls.

Sitting next
to her
I shift

every part
of me
dry

waiting for the canons,
my finger on the musket
trigger, anticipating

how she'll swoon
dodging my bullets,
how she'll drive

us home, explain,
patiently, the plot,
console me; how I'll

envy the chunk
of cheese she'll set out
for that giant rat.

Angels

She grew up
believing
stars were angels,

the night glow
a back-lighting
of security,

a celestial hug;
halos, adornments of gold
for each finger, a toe

ring as an afterthought.
A Gabriel hangs above
her dashboard, a three-inch

pewter Michael guards
her desk with a silver spear,
an androgynous cherub

hugs her neck. I'm pretty
sure she can feel me
at night wrestling next

to Jacob, struggling
to fold my wings
beneath the duvet,

cursing the nightlight
as I search for water,
bend my holy cards.

Vigil

I come to bed
late after
darkness turns

on its backside
and death takes
a cigarette break.

She sleeps face up
still as a museum
piece and I

linger over her
the way we both
used to stare into

the baby's crib,
his fists clenched,
head tilted up

searching for the womb.
I'd hold my palm
above his face, hoping

to catch any small puff
of life as she'd dip closer,
wait for his tiny chest to rise.

Sometimes I couldn't
stand it and I'd poke
him awake for the relief

that came with
his angry cry. Now I
stare down into her

sleeping face, lips
blue-hued, sheen
of night cream, chest

serene, and I panic, reach
until I see movement
behind her eyelids,

realize she's dreaming, cradling
the baby, arranging his
blanket, future. I suspect

she's been staring down at me,
these many long, solo nights
stroking my clenched fists,

naming each breath I've forced
humming prayers and lullabies.
I'm grateful for her fictions, how

they fill the absence, how
she quietly stands in for my shift,
never loses my place.

In the Spirit

Sometimes I see
her ghosts
before she does.

She's always
looking for light,
the outline

of miracles,
a familiar hand
on her shoulder.

I don't believe
in what
I can't kill.

Sometimes I have
to lie, tell her
that earthy, graveyard

smell from my
side of the bed
is my new

after shave.
Sometimes I
can convince her

we're the only
living ones
in the room.

Trash Truck, 7:38 A.M.

We hear different
things. She hears that
powerful engine, screech

of the lifting arm, squeal
of the brakes, and I suspect
she ponders that quarterback

she dated in high school
as she rises, not too quickly,
to gaze out the window.

I forgot to turn
our bin arrows out,
placed said bin too close

to the trees, an impediment
for those giant forked arms.
The trash man must step down

into the street, break his rhythm.
He grabs the green bin, swings
it like an overweight

partner that can't dance,
—our weekly household load—
into that gaping mouth

that grinds and chews
and flips the mess into its
metal belly. I can hear him

swearing as he rolls the empty
bin away from the maple trees.
He shakes his head, throws

a disparaging look toward
the house until he sees her
peek out the window.

She loosens her barrettes,
lets her hair flow
past the sill,

down the new gray siding,
like a curled invitation,
a ladder of perfumed love,

and I hear his smudged
sigh swallowed by his county
engine, feel the vibrations

shake our locked windows.

The Tarantula Counseling Sessions

We learned each
of us has a spider
we keep

hidden, maybe
in a fruit jar,
or as a bracelet;

call it a hobby,
a vice, nail
it on a cross.

Sometimes we
turn it loose
if someone

gets too close,
rifles
through our

drawers, asks
questions
about love.

She buried hers
when she was
young, would

recoil when
it returned,
point it out,

stand behind
me. I'd do my
best to explain

the beauty
of the obsidian
black, red hourglass

of death, diminish
the horror of mine,
its monstrously hairy

legs, swear it only
bites when provoked
or ignored.

Webs are webs
she said after
our first counseling

session, and she
fetched the broom,
grabbed the Raid and I

looked on passively
like I only had two eyes,
no fangs, and all day

to wait and spin
these silky, intricate
love letters.

We Could Be Heroes

She keeps her saints
at a proper distance,
two on the wall, one

in her journal behind
the recipes for liver
pate, meatless chili.

In her hidden drawer,
her heroes; one resembles
her dad, one sports

the dark, Route 66 hair,
another with straight teeth,
and one who looks

like he could change
a fuse in the middle
of the night while

humming, tuck you in.
All my heroes have
Greek and Roman

names. I rewrote
each story, dismantled
the myths, re-arranged

their feats into smaller
annoying poems, changed
the sacrificial altars

into wooden work benches
littered with socket wrenches,
empty coffee cups, sawdust.

I dreamt she sewed
me a blanket for those
long nights on the side

of the mountain, visualizing
her on the half-shell
as I tug on my chain,

humming ancient war dirges,
lighting votive candles,
spying for that eagle.

Drowsy

The dreams,
        prophetic
usually in threes.

There is a symmetry
        on the mystic side
of the curtain.

God likes lines.

Our sleeping daughter
        safe in the radiating
nimbus of her

prayer, the mystery of
        virginity
creeping through her freshman class.

The errant arc
        of our only teenage son,
his paucity of grace,

bad aim,
        indelibly stained
nicotine fingers pinching,

miming the spark-
        plug gap,
that left hand of God.

Once, drunk on
        gin fizzes
she giggled and said:

"Heaven's probably a giant
        family re-union
with no booze."

And I offered something
            about epistles
and apostles, the infinity

of forgiveness,
            drunk monks
scribing by candlelight.

The dreams are
            emphatic
how I unzip my

chest each night
            rummage
 for my soul

how my trembling fingers
            reach
into the wound

            to touch.

Reincarnation For Dummies

Once a queen, I dreamed,
or a kept woman; she's lived
many lives, knows the flutter

of silk across her thigh,
glint of emerald catching
sunlight at a June picnic.

Through the centuries
she found the throne,
took a lover with a crown,

managed a stable of peasants.
Movements shadow
themselves, retrace

the brush of a cheek,
flick of the wrist,
exposure of her rival's neck.

Tonight she is taking
the blade to carrots,
onions, slicing the roast,

hands moving to rhythms
cast in previous lifetimes.
She pours a glass of burgundy,

lifts it to her lips, blesses
the air granting mercy
to the evening and to me.

"I Do" I Said

The arrow of commitment
flies more slowly
when inherited.

Once they smell
fermentation, fruit
flies cluster.

Rice is thrown,
birds perch
like sacrificial lanterns.

Some of the best
days are passive,
she says, quit fussing.

The myth is 50-50:
Love prefers
improper fractions.

Flesh stretches one way
for love, another
for kids.

The first-born son
sleeps between us,
never moves.

This is the stanza for
mythology, Delphi,
allusions to birds, therapy.

She never flinches
as I line up the nails,
not once.

Her sister says, packing,
"You usually divorce for
the same reasons you marry."

She chooses Earth, the twin
daughters, Air & Water;
I smoke alone.

She blesses my man
cave; I never
mention weight.

Her last
love note,
unsigned.

I reinforce
the eyelets
on our 40th

Anniversary banner;
she dusts all
the guests

Thirtieth Anniversary

She dreams
of onyx, I'm
pretty sure,

a holiday beach
in Mexico
with a child

who sells carved
elephants, jingles
pesos, pans

for American gold.
Before she wakes
I rub lotion

on my hands
and feet
as if I were

an apostle,
an awkward
clumsy one

with wrinkled
sandpaper skin,
a long memory.

Curse

The one time
I heard
her swear

at God,
we were
babysitting our nephew,

barely two,
we took
turns clapping

his tiny back
with cupped hands
to loosen the phlegm,

passed him
back and forth
like a broken doll,

curly black hair,
apple red cheeks,
green eyes that stared

into the other
world, and he
only cried once

when I must have
hit his spine
at the wrong angle.

What kind of God
she said
in the car

and she quit
praying, at least
a year and I

watched the sheen
dull on the day-to-day,
felt the world turn

in on its own ugliness,
sat amazed when the tulips
still came up and all

the peaches were plump
and sweet and my prayers
grew me a little crooked, no

warm steady hand to clap
my back, smooth my
brow, help collect the water

to douse the sacrificial
burning pyre beneath
my side of the bed.

Writing

She hears me swear
at my computer, floats
in, turns on the overhead fan.

The blades cut the light
so that she is both shadow
and revelation.

"Just look out
beyond the streets,"
she says.

"All the good words demand a ransom."

I stare and stare,
flowers, trees, cars,
I even stare into the sun.

"No, not up," she says,
laughing. "They don't
fall. Down, they sprout."

And I stare past
the stories into
the earth, mute foreigner

in this garden of
possibility, a stranger
to all these kindred roots.

Looking For My Gardening Shovel

She believes
rabbits
love petunias
even
the white ones.

On a weekend
during pre-season
I rigged a four foot
wooden fence topped
with chicken wire.

We woke one
August morning
all but a half-dozen
petunias beheaded,
stems sadly swaying.

She replanted
the survivors in
a hanging pot
that spins and dangles
above our bed.

Before she falls
asleep she prays:
Rabbits, flowers,
eternity. I open
the bedroom window
for the hawks.

Ed McManis' work has appeared in more than 70 publications including *Coolest American Stories 2025*. His most recent chapbooks are *The Zombie Family Takes a Selfie*, Bottlecap Press, and *Trash Truck 7:38 A.M. (And Other Love Poems)* Finishing Line Press. Forthcoming are the chapbooks, *Decaf with the Philosophers* and *St. Francis Eighth Grade Class of 1971: An Album*. He, along with his wife, Linda, have published esteemed author Joanne Greenberg's (*I Never Promised You a Rose Garden*) memoir, *On the Run*. Little known trivia fact: he holds the outdoor free-throw record at Camp Santa Maria: 67 in a row. He is still married to his first wife, Linda.